The Angel of Christmas

By Arya Donahue

Copyright © 2022 by Arya Donahue.

First printing 2022
Second printing 2023
Third printing 2024

All rights reserved.
No part of this book may be reproduced, stored in a retrieval system, or transmitted in any form or by any means, electronic, mechanical, photocopying, recording or otherwise without permission from the author/publisher.

ISBN: 978-0-9714415-0-7

Cover Design by Cecelia Butler, visionary artist

Naturally You

I am grateful for the contributions of...

Ella and her innocent heart, for sharing and caring and always being there

Russ and Zach Donahue for their contributions

Foreword

This book is offered as an inspiration for families to consider new family traditions for Christmas.

We recommend that you spend time on several evenings reading sections of the book together as a family.

A portion of the proceeds will be donated to:
The Nature Conservancy
Preserve.nature.org

Every Christmas Eve, Jim Marshall reads the nativity story with his wife and children. It's a tradition for their family. As he reads the story, he realizes they have never discussed it. This time, while reading, he wonders if there is something symbolic about the manger, the surroundings, the wise men, and the animals.

He reads, "And she brought forth her firstborn son, wrapped him in swaddling clothes and laid him in a manger because there was no room for them in the inn. And there were in the same country, shepherds abiding in the field, 'keeping watch over' their flocks by night. And lo the angel of the Lord came upon them, and the glory of the Lord shone round about them: and they were sore afraid."

Jim wondered how he might feel If he experienced a visitation by an angel. Little did he know what was to come that very evening.

He continued. "And, lo the angel said unto them, fear not: for, behold, I bring you good tidings of great "Joy, which shall be to all people."

Jim realized that the angel in the nativity story was a messenger. He pondered whether there were different types of angels with different purposes. He decided he would talk with his wife about her perspective on angels. Then, they could discuss what they thought about angels with the children.

He would have to hurry to get to the basement and gather his camera, lighting, and all the equipment needed for the Christmas production, knowing that soon the children would be perched at the top of the stairs, eager to come down to open their presents. They did not like waiting and knew they would have to if their father wasn't prepared to film their reactions. His equipment was state of the art and included recording the sounds of the children's surprise and excitement. Staying behind the camera was where their father, Jim, felt comfortable, but he didn't know that everything would change after their visit with The Angel of Christmas.

Candy and Jack Marshall are privileged children. They live in a beautiful large home and have almost anything they want. Like all children, they looked forward to Christmas morning to see if Santa had brought them everything on their list. Truth be known, they always got more than was on their list.

As Jim set the stage for the production, his wife Ann came down to the kitchen to put the coffee cake in the oven, make coffee, take away the cookies, and empty the glass of milk that had been put on the fireplace for Santa the night before.

Finally, all was ready for the children to come down the stairs. Jim and Ann went to the bottom of the stairs looking up at the children with big smiles of excitement, and said, "Merry Christmas!" Dashing down the stairs with squeals of delight, Jack and Candy came upon the magical living-room scene with the giant Christmas tree sparkling with colored lights, antique ornaments, and ones they had made, surrounded by mounds of presents.

Christmas traditions in the Marshall household included picking a tree and decorating it as a family. On Christmas Eve, they would be allowed to open one present along with the package that included their matching pajamas.

Wrapping paper flew through the air as they opened their presents. A red drum set for Jack drew immediate attention, so he began to play. Five-year-old Candy started with her first box, revealing a porcelain doll with long, curly blonde hair. Candy had seen the baby doll in a local store and wanted her so much! Next, Jack would open his most enormous box. He expressed disappointment as it was not the most expensive gaming system that his best friend John had, which had been attracting Jack's friends to play with John.

Jim had tried to get the game's latest version, which had sold out. With the big presents already opened, her father handed Candy a tiny box. She was delighted with the special attention her father gave her, and she was surprised because her mother usually gave gifts, not her father. Her father worked in his father's jewelry business, and Candy enjoyed going to work with him on occasion and had made many requests to have a diamond. As she pulled away the tissue paper, there was a tiny emerald-cut diamond. Disappointed at the size, she said, "It's too small."

Jim was shocked at what he considered an ungrateful comment by his daughter, so he immediately took the tiny box with the diamond and said, "Alright, if it is too small for you, we will return it".

Candy did not realize that her reaction and her father's response meant that she would not have that diamond, but she would also not have a bigger one or any diamond as a gift from her father again. Candy's comment about the size of the diamond ring, and Jack's disappointment at his most expensive gift, surprised and disturbed their father.

After they opened all the presents, Jim suggested they all go outside and make snow angels, but all the children wanted to do was play with their new gifts. Jack played his drum set in the basement, where he could play without disturbing the adults, and Candy went to her room to play with her beautiful doll.

As Jim and Ann cleaned up all the wrapping paper, they discussed their favorite moments of the children's delight with their presents. Jim was still feeling disturbed by Candy's response to her gift of the diamond and Jack's remark about his disappointment in his device. He asked Ann to sit and sip coffee with him to talk about his concern.

Jim expressed that he was surprised at their children's lack of appreciation for their gifts. In Candy's defense, Ann said she thought their daughter did not understand how expensive a diamond is, and maybe some further explanation of that to Candy would be worthwhile. If she understood that, then there could be a reconsideration of allowing her to have it. Jim was adamant and said it might be a sign that they refocus on so much gift-giving and consider other traditions that would provide a deeper meaning of the true nature of Christmas.

That night after the children went to bed early, so tired from playing with their new toys, Jim and Ann sat by the fireplace to reflect further on the day. They nestled on the couch while snow fell outside. The house was peaceful. They were so relaxed that Jim had decided not to get up and tend the fire even though its flame was growing dim. Suddenly, a glow was getting brighter and brighter from outside the fireplace. Jim and Ann were captivated and speechless as this golden orb of light grew more prominent and closer until an image began to take shape. Then it was as if the entire sphere dissolved, and there in the living room stood a very tall presence with outstretched wings radiating light that covered the room. A profound feeling of pure love emanated. It was as if neither Jim nor Ann could move or speak, and they did not. Instead, they basked in the radiance of this loving presence.

"I am the Angel of Christmas, and I am here to give you a message to set an example for a new Christmas tradition. Humanity has lost its way in the material world, consumed with getting rather than giving, sharing, and caring. This pattern is particularly evident at Christmas, so I have come to ask you to reset and restore the reason for celebrating Christmas.

"The symbols of the nativity at Christmas began with the recognition by wise men guided by a star signifying that a divine essence had come to Earth. Loving parents surrounded the pure innocence of the babe. This babe was lying in the embrace of the natural world. He lay in a manger with hay signifying nature's provision and surrounded by animal kingdom representatives, the camel and donkey symbols of service and humility. The gifts of gold, frankincense, and myrrh represented the purest and most precious essences of the plant and mineral kingdom. Humanity has forgotten that they have come into this world connected to the source of love supported by nature to experience their innocence. They have strayed from their awareness of the awe, beauty, wonder, and healing that nature freely gives.

"Your tradition of bringing the tree inside the house to decorate it and admire it is at a deeper level to acknowledge the beauty of nature. However, trees are living organisms that provide shade, shelter, and nourishment, clean the air, provide oxygen, help prevent soil erosion, and provide sanctuary for animals and birds. Removing them from their natural world is an old paradigm. When we consider how their presence nourishes us, we owe it to them to safeguard a fragile future.

"In the spirit of giving, I wish humanity to become more aware of opportunities to observe and offer kindness to others. The natural world is healing; spending time in nature can be a doorway to restoring divine source connection and joyful purpose. When humanity serves the world through its unique gifts, talents, and humble acts of loving kindness, they fulfill its purpose. With this refocused attention on the deeper meaning of the symbols of the nativity, I ask that you and your family create new traditions that honor and respect the qualities of innocence, humility, thankfulness, service, nature and the animal kingdom."

Astounded, Jim and Ann sat motionless and speechless for several minutes. With the purpose complete, the Angel of Christmas began to disappear into the golden orb as it became brighter and brighter, larger and larger. The vision moved out of the living room, gradually disappearing. Ann turned to Jim with a look of astonishment. All Jim could do was shake his head yes. After a few moments, Ann asked Jim if he had seen what she had seen and felt all the love that she had felt. Jim said he was astonished by the feeling of love and deep peace he had experienced in the presence of this angel. Ann agreed. As they gained their composure, Jim repeated to Ann what he had understood, and Ann admitted that she had heard what Jim had heard. They were to honor Christmas with new traditions that would be new ways of living all year round. The couple decided to gather the children in the morning and discuss these new traditions they would create together.

The children awoke early the following day in a hurry to play with their new gifts. Jim and Ann were already excited about sharing the news with the children. They were waiting at the breakfast table when the children came down. Jim offered to make their favorite blueberry pancake breakfast. The offer of their favorite meal was the only thing that would distract the children from dashing off to play with their new toys. They grabbed their gaming devices before sitting at the table and became engrossed in their worlds.

When Ann came out from the kitchen to bring the juice, she asked them to put their new devices away, and there would be exciting news for them to share as a family. It was obvious that both Jack and Candy were hoping that this family discussion would not take long so they could play with their new presents.

After eating, Jim asked Ann, Jack, and Candy to join him in the living room, where he lit a cozy fire and had paper and pen on the glass coffee table. The children grabbed their devices, hoping they would soon be back to their inner tech worlds. Ann gently asked them to give her their devices which they begrudgingly did, and she took them out of the room.

Ann took her seat beside Jim, and Jack and Candy sat on cushions bearing each of their names, facing their

parents, as the snow continued to fall and the fireplace crackled.

Jim began by saying that he had always enjoyed the Christmas season; but that, particularly during the shopping frenzy over the years, he felt there was too much focus in our society on getting more and more things that lacked significance. The spirit of Christmas no longer seemed to exist. Ann agreed with Jim that the heart of the season had become more about getting presents than focusing on the spiritual principles of giving, sharing, and caring. Ann told the children that she and their father knew that both Candy and Jack were kind and loving and that they appreciated these qualities in both. Ann also said that they knew that they, as well as their friends, had many beautiful things to play with and that, in recent years, it seemed that there was a spirit of not having enough, being unsatisfied, and wanting more.

Jim said he had felt disappointed with the children's responses to their gifts this year. Ann said that while she realized that Candy probably didn't fully understand the expense of a diamond, even a small one; and Jack didn't get the most expensive gaming platform, sadly, there was a lack of appreciation for their gifts. Then Jim began to share the magical story of their visitation with the Angel of Christmas.

"As your mother and I sat by the fire reflecting on our Christmas Day, suddenly, appearing in the room was a ball of brilliant light that kept getting larger and larger. A feeling of love and peace permeated the space, and we were both speechless. Then a form began to take shape from within the ball of light." At this point, the children were both thoroughly captivated by their father's story. As he recounted the experience, the energy of peace and love that the angel brought began filling the space in the living room again.

Jim went on to say that as the form became more explicit and transparent, it began to form the shape of a colossal angel that was as large as their cathedral ceiling, filling the room. It was not a male or female angel, but they knew it was an angel because of its enormous wings. Then the angel began to communicate with them, and Jim shared that the feeling of love and peace in the room grew as the angel conveyed the message.

Then, Jim said the angel explained to them the meaning of the symbols of the nativity and what they represented. Jack spoke up proudly and said they had discussed it in Bible school. "It meant Jesus' birth, and because there were no rooms in the inn when it was time for Jesus to be born, they had to have the delivery in the stable."

He also said, "The three wise men brought presents from their various countries, and a star in the sky showed them the way to Bethlehem."

Jim responded to Jack, saying that although what Jack learned in Bible school was generally accepted, the Angel of Christmas shared a much deeper meaning that was now important for everyone to understand.

Jim told the children that he didn't know if they were the only family that the Angel of Christmas had visited. However, they thought it quite possible that there were others because the angel clarified that humanity had lost its way in patterns of getting rather than giving.

And he said further that the visitation had changed his and his wife's hearts by allowing them to have clarity about their new understanding of the sacred meaning of the symbols of the nativity that could change the hearts of many. Ann noticed that the energy of love and peace was continuing to permeate the room, and she wondered why since the Angel of Christmas was not there. Then she became aware that this energy of peace and love was emanating from the area of her heart, and as she turned her attention to Jim, she felt the surge of energy also emanating from his heart. Ann felt this energy from their hearts as though a beam of light was connecting with their children's hearts. Ann reflected on how the angel's words activated this energy of love and peace in all of their hearts. She realized that now she, Jim, Jack, and Candy would carry this energy in their hearts and share it with others just by telling the story of the meaning of the symbols of the nativity.

Jim continued sharing with the children the request from the angel that their family create new traditions for the celebration of Christmas based on their unique understanding of the symbols of the nativity. He said that this would take heartfelt consideration for each family member, and he asked that Jack and Candy each consider the true meaning of the symbols of the nativity.

As Jim reminded the children of the purpose of creating new traditions, Ann wrote down the true meaning of the nativity symbols for each family member.

Jim said each family member would have a copy of the true meaning of the symbols of the nativity for them to consider. During the month, there would be family meetings to discuss ideas brought by each family member. Over time they would create their new Christmas traditions based on acknowledging the divine spark in each person, remembering our innocence, sharing, caring, and respecting the natural world and animal kingdom.

The children took a few minutes to speak as Jim finished the story, with the family surrounded in a cocoon of love and peace. Candy said that she could feel herself wanting to share the feeling she had just experienced with everyone, including the trees, as living beings that she loved so much. Jack said he realized he felt silly having so many Christmas gifts knowing that many children don't have any. Jack and Candy agreed they were excited to create new family Christmas traditions.

As Jim drove to work, he realized that each time he thought about the visitation of the Angel of Christmas, he would feel enfolded by the same presence of love. He had also become aware that when he thought about the experience with the Angel while he was with other people, they also seemed affected by what Jim felt as a softening of their interactions to a kinder way of being. And Jim knew that his way of being with his family was different; he felt more engaged at ease and present with each of them. He now no longer felt the need to be the camera man when special moments were happening with his family members; rather he wanted to be with them experiencing their love, joy and even sorrow.

Jack had always enjoyed the family trips to Chicago to visit their grandparents. He loved the tall buildings and big trucks and, after visits, would try to recreate them with his erector sets. As they entered the town, Jack noticed two people carrying large bags behind them. He noticed that their clothes looked tattered and worn. Jack asked his father why they were carrying big bags behind them.

His father said, "These are homeless people."

Jack asked why they did not have homes, and his father replied that life circumstances, maybe a loss of a job, or addiction to a drug or mental health issues, had brought them to living on the streets and finding food wherever they could. He said that while there are shelters where homeless people can go for food, more people need places than are available. Jack had never felt sadness like this before in his heart. He did not realize that the powerful energy of love, which came when his parents shared the story of their experience of the visitation with the Angel of Christmas, had touched his heart. At that moment, Jack knew his new Christmas family tradition.

Candy always loved to swing on her swing set in the backyard by the prominent Dutch elm tree, which her mother told her was the guardian grandmother tree of their property among the other Dutch elms. It seemed like hours would go by as she went as high as she could singing "Zip-a-Dee-Do-Dah." She had heard her mother sing this song for as long as she could remember. It made Candy feel happy and free. On this day, as she was enjoying her swing time, she heard a loud buzzing sound that went on and on, disturbing her singing. Candy finally decided to stop swinging as the noise kept on. When she got in the house, Candy asked her mother what the loud buzzing noise was. Ann replied that a disease was affecting the Dutch elm trees, and the trees affected were being cut down.

Candy was shocked as she thought of her friend, the Dutch elm, that held a significant place next to her swing set. She would often nestle herself in the warm spot where the big limbs came together in the grand guardian tree on their property. With tears welling up in her tiny eyes, she asked, "Mommy, are they going to cut down grandmother tree that we love so much?"

Ann knew this was a delicate moment for her daughter and that she would need to be conscientious about sharing this news. "No, honey, grandmother tree is well, although the Dutch elm which is outside your bedroom window will have to come down so that it will not affect grandmother tree."

"Oh no!" cried Candy, as she would often awake with the sun shining on the beautiful tree outside her window. Candy remembered a story her teacher told her class on Arbor Day about a man in India who planted 38,000 trees in 28 years. Candy began to have the feeling in her heart that she first felt when her father was telling the story of the visitation of The Angel of Christmas, and she knew now what her new Christmas family tradition would be.

Ann loved writing small poems for her relatives and friends on birthdays. It was something that seemed to come naturally to her. At least two Saturdays per month, and on most holidays, Ann would visit her great-aunt in an assisted-living home. Ann had become more aware of how few visitors were coming to see other residents on her visits. On her next visit to her great- aunt, Ann became aware of the feeling in her heart that she had felt when the Angel of Christmas visited her and her husband, and immediately Ann knew what her new Christmas tradition would be.

Jim's grandfather Walt and his brother Sam had spent their early childhood living in an orphanage after their father died; and their mother, an emigrant from Scotland, had no way to care for them. Jim recalled stories his grandfather would tell him about how he and his brother looked so forward to a visit from their mother, who would bring them a candy bar each visit. After some of Jim's grandmother's relatives joined her in this country, his grandfather and brother could leave the orphanage, go to school, and become successful businesspeople.

After his grandfather's history of living in an orphanage that closed in the mid-1900s, Jim paid attention to the care of children. He discovered that foster care had become a fundamental way of caring for these children. Recently, Jim had become aware that there had been a return to providing residential treatment homes for children and group-care facilities in the past several years. A friend had told him of a non-profit organization whose mission is to create a positive mentality for kids in crisis through the compassionate power of a helping hand. As Jim thought of this organization, the warm feeling he first felt during the visitation of the Angel of Christmas returned, and he knew what his new Christmas tradition would be.

It had been a month since Christmas and the experience with the Angel of Christmas. Each family member had kept their ideas to themselves. Now it was time for them to have a family meeting to share their ideas with each other to create their new family traditions.

They had enjoyed their favorite blueberry pancake breakfast, and everyone felt an excitement about spending time together with this new project. But during the past month there had been evidence of family members demonstrating new behaviors. At meals they picked a message card from a bowl that had a certain inspirational message like: being grateful, being trustworthy, being empowered. Each family member would take a turn sharing what the way of being meant to them. Jack and Candy no longer dashed off right after meals; rather, they helped clear the table.

As they gathered in the living room by the fireplace, each one shared their ideas. Jim would be involved with the foster-care organization as a volunteer, Ann offered poetry writing at the assisted-living facility, Candy wanted to plant a tree each year on Arbor Day, and Jack wanted to volunteer to serve meals at the homeless shelter.

Jim and Ann expressed to Jack and Candy how much they respected their willingness to be aware of ways that they could be more caring and that their newly-adopted ways of being more helpful and kind to each of their family members were noticed and appreciated.

They decided that the entire family would share in the new tradition of not cutting down a Christmas tree but rather decorating the one that was just outside the living room window. Each year at Christmas time they would display and share the true meaning they had learned from the Christmas Angel. As a family they decided to go to the homeless shelter in the afternoon and serve food as well as go to the assisted- living facility and sing Christmas carols. And finally, they would each be given a certain amount of money to buy a present for a child at the foster-care facility.

With these new traditions agreed upon, they all decided to go outside and make Christmas Angels in the snow.

Now you and your family are offered this same opportunity to create new Christmas traditions based on these principles: acknowledging the divine spark in each person, remembering our innocence, sharing, caring, and respecting the natural world and the animal kingdom. Symbols of the nativity shared from the heart will be felt in the hearts of others.

Arya Donahue

Our new Christmas family traditions:

www.ingramcontent.com/pod-product-compliance
Lightning Source LLC
Chambersburg PA
CBHW061817290426
44110CB00026B/2892